RUN FOR YOUR LIFE

ISBN 978-1-62462-166-6

Copyright © 2018 by Scott F. Parker

RUN FOR YOUR LIFE

A MANIFESTO

Scott F. Parker

We do not disagree about the purpose of human life.

We disagree only about how to achieve it.

May I suggest running?

Run for your life.

There is no running but for your life.

Either you are chasing your next meal; or you are escaping danger; or, just as significantly, you are creating meaning.

We are beings toward meaning.

What makes us human?

This.

Can one fail one's humanity?

If one fails in this.

Will running help you live longer?

Wrong question.

Will it help you live better?

Do you wish to be thinner or healthier or fitter for soccer? Is the point to look good naked?

Very well. Your life is your own. So are your priorities.

But running that is merely instrumental isn't really running.

Like a sprinter, hold nothing back: you're doing it wrong.

Run like your body makes the rules. Run like a child. Run like evolution has a telos and that telos is you. Run like Steve Prefontaine is whispering in your ear. Run like there is no future because there isn't. Run like you are a destiny. Run like Usain Bolt smiles. Run like Allyson Felix—or water down a mountainside. Run like your legs, your stride, your rhythm, your pace, your endurance are all the world knows. Run like you'd be happy to watch yourself if you weren't happier being yourself.

How far can you go?
You can go farther.

How fast can you go?
You can go faster.

How beautiful?
More beautiful.

How happy?
Happier.

Alive?
Yes.

Meaning?
All of it.

Meaning in these godless times, how can it be so? Meaning is made on the ground, the author on the move. Motionlessness the only oblivion, true stillness lies in the center of movement, the mass point of the soul—*if there is such a thing it is this*.

Running, there is neither past nor future, only the present moment created one breath, one stride at a time. This is called finding one's purpose. Or embracing every moment that led to this one.

As usual, Prefontaine says it best: *Some people create with words or with music or with a brush and paints. I like to make something beautiful when I run. I like to make people stop and say, "I've never seen anyone run like that before." It's more than just a race, it's a style. It's doing something better than anyone else. It's being creative.*

Not all runners are fast.

And not all who are fast are runners.

But all those whose most absorbed and passionate hours are spent turning legs over ground—*these are runners*.

Headphones are for those who don't trust their own minds; who fear solitude; who believe avoiding thinking about death means avoiding death; who think reality is merely their thoughts; who don't know they're already dead; who have no business running. Let them sleep. Leave the running to us.

If you have to look at your watch to find out if you're happy you deserve every curb you trip over.

Run when you feel like running. Rest when you feel like resting. Don't ask too many questions, and don't read too many books. The bones in your feet are smarter than the thoughts in your mind or the advice of your coach. Before all else, cultivate the ability to listen to bones.

I believe in culture and cultivation, but
culture will never know more than your legs,
and you will never be more cultivated than
while you're on the run.

Feelings are feelings and thoughts are thoughts. But feelings produce thoughts and thoughts produce feelings.

So when you listen to your body know what language it is speaking.

Why didn't evolution produce the wheel?

There isn't a mountain my legs can't climb.

From time to time the runner will see god on the mountaintop.

When she does she gives a subtle nod and continues on her way.

There are no accomplishments in running.

The only goal: to continue running.

The runner thinks in miles and sunrises. In surface conditions and air quality.

When the air is bad the runner is the first to sense it.

Life is objectively meaningless. So don't live your life objectively. Live subjectively. Place yourself at the center of your experience.

I can see your pointless life, reader, one of billions in one lonely solar system. Birth, death, all the rest between. To what end? To what value? Reality happening and happening all around, us dragged along with it, helpless.

So what? I am no different. Except that I run. And when I run meaninglessness flees from me like a shadow from the light.

Look directly at the nothingness of your existence and chase it away.

My run is meaningful to me because it is *my* run. I need run no other race than that.

If you tell me being on a treadmill is just as good as running you might as well tell me that pornography is just as good as sex. And if you insist that this is the world we live in now I will insist *it doesn't have to be*.

Have I gone too far?

The runner goes too far, then goes farther.

Who I am to tell you you don't know how to live?

A runner.

Just as the body withers in the chair it wasn't built for, so the mind withers in the body at rest.

Your god is dead.
Your planet is dying.
Your nation is in decline.
Your friends are hostage to their idiot-devices.
Perhaps all of it is ending.
Nevertheless, in the meantime, you can still run.

It is a good thing sometimes to run yourself to boredom, especially if you see it through to the other side.

Running isn't a sport, it's a personality trait.
   One that is cultivated.
I've heard not everyone can be a runner.
   Good!
Not everyone can be a physicist, a thinker,
   an artist.
Look around you—how many will flourish?
It means something to be a runner.
It means pain but not suffering
It means being unashamed of one's body—
   unashamed of *being* that body.
It means living in one's own skin—burned,
   blistered, coated in dirt.
It means learning all the surfaces and where
   they make contact.

Was I born to run?

Were you?

Running is play.
Look at children.
Look at anyone of refined taste.
For an adult to run freely takes cultivation
 or youthfulness—either way exuberance.
If it's not fun you're not doing it right.

We runners are not afraid to say what we know. There are higher and lower tastes, higher and lower persons. No runner is a utilitarian.

Running through the streets is better than running on a track. And running on the beach or in the woods is better still. Running on a treadmill is not running at all. If this is "just how you like to run," you are not one of us.

Running, one hears one's own ideas. There are no one else's. Your best ideas—your best *self*—emerges on a run. So be smart yourself: take a hammer to your idiot-device.

If you won't, if you *can't*, then put this book down before it burns you.

If running is suffering it's not running.

If running brings you suffering you are not hard enough to be a runner.

Pain—the runner knows from good and bad. Good pain is the feeling of getting stronger. Bad pain is the feeling of not being strong enough.

And good pain is like no pain—it is freedom first.

Until running is made punishment and work, it is play.

And it can be play again.

And it always was.

Life should be a downhill run.

And the true runner runs uphill like he runs downhill.

Go to your local marathon. Pick a spot after the twenty-mile mark. At around four hours you'll see the first runner who didn't know to use bandages over his nipples, or who forgot to, or who remembered to put them on but sweated them off hours ago. Look up from the bloody streaks running down his shirt and if you have the right angle look in his eyes. Do you recognize that emotion? Have you made its acquaintance?

Vaseline between your thighs and all over your toes, laces double knotted, shirt removed, visor secured, shorts as short as they'll go, sunscreen applied liberally, bowels evacuated beyond doubt, sinews and muscles loose, bones unbreakable, the mind along for the ride.

The point of running is not to get somewhere.

Nor is it to necessarily go fast or far.

The point of running is to be free. To always be falling and never hit the ground.

It can only be about one thing—everything reduces to this—there can be nothing else—there is only—we experience only—we are for no purpose but: *the joy of running qua running*.

In whatever we do, our ends must always be greater than our means.

For some, running is a means to some other end, but the runner doesn't live in this world, has no interest in ever visiting. For him running is an end in itself. That is, the experience is the thing. Whatever gives to it is good, whatever takes from it is bad—this is his morality. The experience is multifaceted. Sometimes it is pain. Sometimes it is bliss. Sometimes it is even boredom. Always it is his highest calling.

The runner has nothing to prove to no one. He sleeps on the hard ground or in a luxurious bed without complaint. He's easy. In fact, it's entirely likely that he's not sleeping at all. No, he's outside right now, this very moment, running. Right now? you ask. To be sure. Look out the window. There he went.

Running is only a word for something about the human being in the same way that *thinking* is a word about the human being. Our essence is a negotiation between what we can and what we do.

Mind, body, and *soul*—more words, more miles we can cover if we start now.

The runner isn't an *embodied* being. She isn't *in* her body; she's *of* her body. And when she runs she runs not as her body but as her *being*.

What does he eat, this runner?

He eats whatever he wants. Usually plants—nuts and fruit. He likes breads and cheeses. Salt and sunlight. When he eats meat he eats it raw, the blood on his hands.

You watch your loved ones decline and suffer and die as you follow the same trajectory at your own rate. You have no faith in resurrection—no interest in it either. If someone offered you an afterlife or immortality you'd decline. This life is enough for you. It is meaningless only until you come along. If there were a god and he gave you meaning when he gave you life, it would be no good. You earn your own meaning one mile at a time. The meaning that is given to you is self-defeating. In a godly universe there is no meaning. It takes an ungodly universe for the runner to become his own god and make his own meaning.

In a trail race I was running, the runner in front of me, coming to a high mountain vista, stretched his arms out wide and yelled, "Thank you, Jesus. This is beautiful."

As I passed him I said, "How about this? If I beat you in this race, there's no God. If you beat me, there is."

"It doesn't work like that," he said.

Exactly.

The runner doesn't stop until the run is over.

And even then he is only pausing until the next run begins.

What about you? You are thinking of taking up running. Is it a good idea?

No. This way of being is not yours.

The bird flies, the fish swims, and the runner runs.

It is not so easy to breathe in these stupid times.

Running clears the lungs.

The runner is not a religious man. He knows enough history not to believe in progress. His faith is in his legs. But only for the time being.

In a life wherein education prepares you to work prepares you to retire prepares you to die without ever having lived, the beauty of running is that it serves no purpose whatsoever—save the most important one: purposelessness. It is only there that one might find *lasting* meaning.

The paradox: We are not chasing a time, a distance, another runner. We are not chasing experience or even meaning. We simply, stupidly, *just* run. And in this way only do we achieve what we're after.

After a marathon—or even a hard 5K—the stresses of modern life, for a little while, take their proper place. Career insecurity, social anxiety, shame, regret—what are these to an animal breathing deeply, sweating, pumping, overcoming?

At the end of the day—no, at the beginning of the day, all day long: we are animals, bodies loose upon the earth.

We are atoms, too, or quarks, strings, *whatever*. Let's go farther and say reality as we experience it is a simulation or at its most basic level information. This matters to the runner not at all.

Prefontaine ran to win, of course. But more than that he ran to impose his will. On his competitors, on his spectators, on the universe itself—and the long, dark death he knew was coming for him.

Nihilism stalks the weak. No one who watched Prefontaine race ever despaired again. In his tailwind we all race.

We may run with our wills and some of us will triumph before we fail. But we may also run with our beings and bypass the terms of triumph and failure. We may run, as it were, our own races, which are not races at all. We are not giving up. We are giving up the notion that there is anything to give up.

We are not infinite beings. The runner knows her limits, knows them in her muscles and her bones, in her lungs and her heart, in her imagination and her courage. And she is grateful for these limits; without them, running would be as meaningless as immortality.

There are no abstractions in running, no big ideas. There are only facts in running, details: the way your feet strike the ground; the way your foot feels the cracks and rocks and rolls around them; the way your ankle flexes on uneven ground; the way your arms, legs, and heart pump in harmony; the way your legs propel you forward—and catch you too; the way your arms carry you over a climb; the way your fists unclench and stress becomes impossible to hang onto; the way your center of gravity never jostles; the way your lungs fill and empty in an easy rhythm; the way your gaze falls soft and steady; the way you forget if you're making an effort; the way you don't want to stop.

Running is not a recklessness, but it is a wildness. Kant could not ever have been a runner. But Nietzsche and Thoreau—those other great walkers—might easily have run: their world is the one at their feet. If they had written like Kant they'd have fallen on their faces.

The path the runner follows is wide and he widens it with every step.

And where there is no path before him, there is one behind him.

The runner does not turn back from new routes, new directions, *new selves*.

The runner is one who knows that at his core is a void, his essence is essencelessness.

He does not *discover* himself through running, he expands himself, *creates* himself.

The patterns she learns are hers to violate.

The way between A and B is the way she takes, no other.

And when she finds herself midway it is neither coming nor going that defines her but the being, for now, here and, now, already gone.

The route I most often run now follows a small stream south from the pond near my house. After three quarters of a mile I turn onto a straight suburban street that leads me to a larger pond. There, my path follows the northern edge of the water, passing through a small woods, where fishermen cast and young lovers hold each other discreetly. Continuing on, I follow a path north through neighborhoods. A wooden footbridge spans another stream in a small grassland between housing developments. From there the path wends between backyards and parks before it dumps me on the street I live on and I have a straight shot a mile and a half past the school, the church, the creek where I began, the mountains in the distance, the sweat on my skin, the sunshine all around me.

Running is what we do when we forget not to.

It is the way our body wants to move.

It is how we find ourselves when ideas aren't getting in the way of happiness.

The runner resonates with his surroundings.

He imposes no will, leaves no trace, conquers nothing.

He moves, reacts, adapts, continues.

A run doesn't lead one to the end of the run.

Passing here is not a means to reaching there.

You don't eat once, breathe once, have sex once and call it good, cross *that* off your to-do list.

Running is how your body smiles. And how it gives thanks.

An unread book, an unworn sweater, a potential unrealized.

Let us be grateful and use what we receive.

These legs: *they run!*

In the same way that Chuang Tzu's True Man can enter water without getting wet and fire without getting burned, the runner, when he ceases to fight himself, can run without tiring.

Through running, the runner learns of life.

As his foot meets the uneven ground in the morning with adaptability, so too his mood meets unplanned circumstances in the evening with equanimity.

What is virtue? Doing the right thing at the right time in the right way.

What is *right*? The cultivation of judgement.

How do we cultivate? Practice. Experience. Exposure. Adaptability.

The runner, if only when she runs, knows where each step should fall.

These higher things—these *values*—do they lie on a mountain or in a meadow?

There are as many routes as there are runners.

Only at the summit do they converge.

And when you reach the summit, what do you see below?

All the miles you've come, all the miles still to go.

What would a runner do, I ask myself.

The answer is always the same: whatever the moment requires. Often this is to move, sometimes it is to stay still, always it is to know which, forever it is to know how to know: to know how to listen, to know how to hear the sound before it is made: to comprehend one's circumstances, and within them to create: to be!

The runner doesn't believe in discipline.

Discipline is for the weak.

Instead, he believes in passion, enthusiasm, joy, celebration, and whims—the divine madness of his whims!

Is the runner a mystical figure?

Is the archer? The butcher? The Buddha?
The dancer? The poet?

He is out there somewhere, up ahead.

You must catch him before you can speak to him.

But if you are out of breath when you reach him there will be nothing for you to say.

The runner loves the rain, the snow, the wind.
She loves the sun and the moon.
She loves the uphill, the downhill, and the level ground.
She loves the morning and the night.
She makes judgements only where judgements bring her more fully to life.

The runner is not afraid of the noontime sun.

He has nothing to hide.

He comes from the sun, he goes to the sun.
Without shame.

The runner values all things, some more than others.

She would be the one to claim there is no joy
    like a fifty-five-degree rainstorm.
The puddles.
The drippy trees.
The soggy leaves.
The spongy aspect of socks.
The way skin wants to be wet.
The way we can always be cleansed.

It's not that he doesn't see you there.

He does.

And there are things he would say to you.

It's just that he does not have the time to say them.

So sorry, he could add but doesn't.

Memento mori, as the rock gives way.
Memento mori, as the ankle turns over.
Memento mori, as the bushes rustle.
Memento mori, as the legs wobble.
Memento mori, as the lungs burn.
Memento mori, as the mind leaks away.
Memento mori, as one revolution becomes
    the next.
Memento mori, as the surface of a large
    enough circle appears flat.

Everything the runner sees she sees from the perspective of her own eyes bouncing along over her own feet. Nothing for her is unearned or inaccessible.

The runner writes his own script.

He is breaking new ground.

Not even he knows where his route will lead.

The story is always chasing at his heels, never able to close the gap, as the runner never hesitates.

In times of lies, the runner knows the truth.

One needn't believe in god or progress to know truth.

Running, there are no lies.

How to be a runner: don't ask how to be a runner.

The being is in the doing.

The runner is in the running.

The worldview: sedentary life isn't.

The value: the experience.

Better: the practice.

Home: on your feet, on the move, right now.

Rest: when you must.

Run: ditto.

Advice: be as cautious of caution as of risk.

Imagine that you are diagnosed with a
condition whose symptom is regular
suffering relieved only by death.

Now, tell me your response.

Run for your life.

We are as we ever were: *beings toward meaning*.

It is possible still at this late date to become human.

www.ingramcontent.com/pod-product-compliance
Lightning Source LLC
Chambersburg PA
CBHW011801040426
42449CB00016B/3462